A Prophetic Word for Entering the New Era

THE END
OF THE
WORLD
as we know it

JOHNNY ENLOW

pronouns in Scripture that refer to the Father, Son, and Holy Spirit, and may differ from some publishers' styles.

DESTINY IMAGE® PUBLISHERS, INC.

P.O. Box 310, Shippensburg, PA 17257-0310

"Promoting Inspired Lives."

This book and all other Destiny Image and Destiny Image Fiction books are available at Christian bookstores and distributors worldwide.

Cover design by: Eileen Rockwell

For more information on foreign distributors, call 717-532-3040.

Reach us on the Internet: www.destinyimage.com.

ISBN 13 TP: 978-0-7684-5680-6

ISBN 13 eBook: 978-0-7684-5668-4

For Worldwide Distribution, Printed in the U.S.A.

1 2 3 4 5 6 7 8 / 24 23 22 21 20

Contents

Introduction

As I write this late in March 2020, we're in the midst of the COVID-19 pandemic (as declared by the World Health Organization). The world has never been shut down in this kind of way, with many nations under total lockdown or quarantine. Despair is rampant. Many are already cursing 2020 after initially being hopeful about it. Our national economy seems at great risk. By extension, that puts the whole world at risk. Some are saying that a new Great Depression, worse than the first one, lies before us. Fear and anxiety have been pumped into already challenging circumstances by a sinister mainstream media—more intent on overthrowing

President Trump than seemingly anything else. The worst-case scenario of millions of deaths and the whole world being thrown into poverty and despair is being projected by many purported experts.

The church is responding and reacting in various ways to these unprecedented challenges and the jury is still out on how we're doing. The usual suspects have come out of the woodwork declaring this is the end. Jesus is coming. The antichrist is here. The Great Tribulation is upon us. Prepare to suffer. Prepare to die. You ain't seen nothing yet—worse is on its way. The Rapture is right around the corner. Some sort of end-time scenario always gets broadcast from the church when we experience a significant challenge.

This book is meant to speak to us right in the midst of all of this, as well as perhaps serve as a reminder when we encounter future scenarios. What I'm going to share is what I've been sharing. What I'm going to prophesy is what I've been prophesying. Nothing that we have experienced or will experience has changed the hopeful and hope-filled forecast for planet earth. Some nations will step into this sooner than others, but a better day is straight ahead. Root systems are being addressed. Things that need to be shaken are being shaken. The Kingdom of God is rushing in and it's not coming into a vacuum. It's displacing and replacing. It's disruptive. It involves the demolition of what's been ruling and the connected structures that were created for sinister purposes.

We've become familiar with and even embraced many of these dark structures. To the degree we're too entangled with them, to that same degree there may be momentary pain for us as we become extricated. Losses can be quickly overcome as we step into the new. A whole new day with almost infinite possibilities is upon us. As 2020 advances, we'll become more and more aware of that. In fact, this is the Great Awakening that so many have announced—it's just being preceded by a rude awakening!

As you read this book of substantive hope, you'll accelerate your own participation in Promised Land realities. Even though God has been speaking into this day for some time, the transition into it required a season of shock and a season of shaking for us all. Without a doubt this is the reality of the day.

Chapter 1

The End of the World as We Know It

In the early stages of the "pandemic" I released the following prophetic word:

> No matter what happens over the next few hours and days—everyone remain calm. This is not the end, but only the end of the world as we know it. This is not the beginning of the tribulation, but it's the beginning of a severe tribulation for the corrupt elite. This is not when Christ comes to take us home—it's when Christ is coming to judge advanced evil

and establish those who are His
and the plan that is His.

Not only is this not the end, but this is
barely the beginning of the Kingdom age.
In this age the church will learn that the
King and His Kingdom come together. It's
not just about getting eternal security, but
about receiving and showcasing His way of
doing things in every sphere or mountain
of society. We're not yet even comparative two-year-olds in this assignment. The
church has been in an arrested development
period, brought on by trying to leave the
planet before we showcase the Kingdom.
We thought that just telling of the King was
enough, but the King is inseparable from
His Kingdom. "Seek ye first the Kingdom."

What Do the Scriptures Tell Us?

One of the reasons we continually cry our
own version of "Wolf! Wolf!" every time

something foreboding seems to be in play is that we have operated under a distorted narrative—that bad things are the sign that Jesus is returning soon. I've studied and researched it well and every single generation since Paul the apostle has thought they were in some version of "the end" because every generation has faced serious challenges. This end-times mindset (I call it end-times-itis) has always existed. In all of my research I haven't found even one generation that was free of it.

For the last two thousand years, every follower of Jesus has been able to hear or read Revelation 22:12 that says, *"Behold, I am coming soon"* (ESV), and many have thus justified their "end-times-itis." They then add 2 Peter 3:12, "anticipate and hasten the coming of the Lord," as their inspiration.

You may think, "How could they be wrong? It's in the Bible. It's in the Word."

Also in the Word were the wise words of King Solomon in Ecclesiastes 3:1-2 beginning with, *"There is a time for everything, and a season for every activity under the heavens"* (NIV). It goes on to further explain itself, *"a time to be born and a time to die, a time to plant and a time to uproot"*—and then on and on. Can you imagine building a casket for a newborn before they ever live their life just because it's "in the Word"? Can you imagine pulling up a plant right after planting it in order to fulfill Scripture?

The most important thing to know and the hardest thing to know of every prophetic possibility of Scripture is the "when?" The error of every generation has been to try to make the most advanced end-time scenarios of the Bible fit into their day. Beware of that now. Beware of that tomorrow.

The Lord has provided two key helps to assist us with the "when" of things. First is the Holy Spirit. Jesus plainly told us in John 16:13 that He, the Holy Spirit, would show us "things to come." This acknowledges that timing would not come from studying the Bible alone. We need the Holy Spirit to reveal timing. Second, Amos 3:7 says, *"Surely the Sovereign Lord does nothing without revealing his plan to his servants the prophets"* (NIV). This is how we are to process our understanding of "when."

If you've been following reputable prophets during this season, you'll note they're not prophesying present-day challenges as the end. Yes, there are always false prophets, fake prophets, and sometimes just scared communicators who pass a false narrative and timing on to others. Some of them sell thousands and even millions of books. However, only the Holy Spirit and God-sanctioned prophets are going to lead you into the proper Kingdom narrative of the day. His Holy Spirit and His prophets will *always* release hope. That is your guardrail for recognizing truth.

No man, including Jesus, actually knows anything other than the general season of His return (see Matt. 24:36). His instruction for us was not, "Speculate until I come." It was *"Occupy till I come"* (Luke 19:13 KJV). When we combine that instruction with the aforementioned 2 Peter 3:12, "anticipate and hasten the coming of the Lord," we can deduce that us not properly "occupying" could actually lead to His *delay* in coming. If we can hasten His coming, then it's logical or even self-evident that we can delay His coming.

It's important to remember these three Scriptures—their fulfillment precedes His coming:

> *For the earth will be filled with the knowledge of the glory of the Lord, as the waters cover the sea* (Habakkuk 2:14).

> *Arise, shine; for **your** light has come! And the glory of the Lord is risen upon **you**. For behold, the darkness shall cover the earth, and deep darkness the people; but the Lord will arise over **you**, and His glory will be seen upon **you**. The Gentiles shall come to your light, and kings to the brightness of **your** rising* (Isaiah 60:1-3).

Whom heaven must receive **until** the times of restoration of all things, which God has spoken by the mouth of all His holy prophets since the world began (Acts 3:21).

When we read these Scriptures together we understand that one day the whole earth will know (be fully aware and have access to) the truth—not just that Jesus saves, but all of the other aspects of His glory, His goodness, kindness, and love. The entire world (as the waters cover the sea—completely) will know of the glory or beauty and splendor of His ways in every sphere of society. Isaiah 60 makes it clear that He is not first rapturing us or in any way removing or hiding us first, but that we will be the carriers of this multidimensional expression of the glory and goodness of God. We will shine in the seven mountains of culture. We will shine in media, education, government, arts and entertainment, economy, family, as well as in religion. There will be so much light on us that nations will be transformed and the leaders of nations will be sustained by the bright light that we carry and function with in the midst of darkness.

This Acts passage helps us to not prematurely expect Jesus' return. Heaven is going to hang on to Jesus *until* certain things have been accomplished on earth. It's not about a date—it's about a finished assignment. What is that assignment? The assignment is the restoration of all things spoken of by His servants the prophets since the world began—not just the self-proclaimed prophets of the day who find "the end" at every turn or every curious moon phenomenon, but all the prophets of old who addressed end-times matters. Isaiah and Habakkuk were two prophets who were clearest on what had to happen *first*. We are accelerating toward Habakkuk 2:14 and Isaiah 60. Again, this is not the end—just the end of the world as we know it.

Chapter 2

There Is a Storm, but We're Crossing Over

It can be greatly disorienting to be in a storm—especially so when key information about the storm is absent. Generally, we're able to prepare, endure, and outlast a storm by knowing how strong it is and how long it will last. Without that information we are ripe for all sorts of panic and misinterpretation of the storm. Most storms, when processed in the midst of the storm itself, tend to feel like they'll last forever and/or that they'll lead to our destruction. With the global pandemic of a virus and accompanying fears related to the economy, we are in such a storm. Even as this storm passes and we see God's redemption and restoration, we can expect, of course, there will always be more storms. Let's learn in the midst of this one what we can carry with us into the future.

Mark 4:35-41 tells about a storm that Jesus and His disciples encountered on the Sea of Galilee. It's relevant to know (as all who've been to Israel would know) that crossing over the Sea of Galilee is a quick process. It's actually a smallish lake and not a sea at all. Verse 35 starts out with Jesus speaking to His disciples by the Sea of Galilee, saying, *"Let us cross over to the other side."* This is a very important phrase to remember and is highly applicable to us today. We're in a storm that seems to have interrupted our "crossing over," but it hasn't.

As Jesus and the disciples crossed the Sea of Galilee, a great storm suddenly came upon them. The New International Version of verse 37 says, *"A furious squall came up and the waves broke over the boat, so that it was nearly swamped."* *Squall* and *swamped* are such an interesting choice of words for those who have been paying attention to behind-the-scene things going on in our world today related to the "deep state" (organized, long-standing darkness in high places). As the story unfolds, Jesus is asleep in the stern and the disciples are panicked because He seems impervious to the very real storm that's filling their boat with water.

What Did Jesus Say Before the Storm?

The next verse says, *"Jesus was in the stern, sleeping on a cushion"* (NIV). Jesus is all the way in the back of the boat and He's not only sleeping, but sleeping on a cushion. Ever been in a storm of life where it feels like Jesus isn't just asleep, but quite comfortable in His sleep?

The disciples manage to awaken Jesus with, *"Don't you care if we drown?"* (NIV). This wasn't merely a fear attack, but it was a set of circumstances accompanied with an irrational fear. We've seen that in this season as well. Why do I say it was an irrational fear? First of all, they could see Jesus and He was with them. Second, this whole thing started with Him saying, "We are crossing over." When Jesus prophesies, He should be believed. Remember, He does nothing without first prophesying it. This is an important insight for us today.

Jesus had said, "We are crossing over." He rebuked their pitiful faith for forgetting the last thing He had said. Today's application is that if you want to make it through this present global storm and future ones, the most important thing for you to remember is what Jesus was saying—to you personally and through His prophetic voices—before the storm started. We came into 2020 with a consensus of established prophetic voices speaking of an unparalleled breakthrough in so many ways related to economic matters, justice matters, reformation matters, family matters, and the Great Awakening. What was true before the coronavirus-related storm is still true—even if your boat is filling with water and the waves are overwhelming.

In the midst of a storm is not the best time to be processing life or even the storm itself. In a storm you can be anchored by the last directive words of Him who sleeps in and has authority over the storm. Jesus awakened and rebuked the storm itself, but not before chastising the disciples' missed opportunity to grow in faith. Let's learn from their example, and when we go through storms let's respond heroically and in faith instead. We will see our promised destination.

Believe the Prophets of Hope

> *Believe in the Lord your God, and you shall be established; believe His prophets, and you shall prosper* (2 Chronicles 20:20).

This has been perhaps the most repeated prophetic Scripture of 2020 by multiple prophetic voices. I've spoken of it many times myself. Clearly God highlighted this verse for this year because we would be required to live it out. In this Old Testament story, the specific prophet they were instructed to listen to was Jahaziel who, earlier in verse 15, had said, *"Do not be afraid nor dismayed because of this great multitude, for the battle is not yours, but God's."*

Jahaziel means "He who looks to God and God watches over." Lest we forget, 2 Chronicles 20 was not just about prospering because they listened to a prophet. In this scenario, the people were surrounded by immense and unbeatable armies (Moabites, Ammonites, and others) that brought great fear, even to King Jehoshaphat. The setting was very challenging and it was the storm of their day. Today we face a pandemic virus/fear, a challenged economy, a corrupt deep state, and all together they are greater than us.

The right response of that day based on the revelation of the prophet was to have a battalion of worshipers lead them onto the battlefield—where they needed to show up, but not fight. Though we highlight praise as a weapon against the enemy, we often miss that the enemy is primarily fear and not necessarily the surrounding army we find ourselves facing. The awesome end of the 2 Chronicles 20 story is that, as the people subjugated their fears by worshiping and praising God, the Lord caused the enemy to turn on each other and destroy themselves. God will do the same for us as we discern and then heed present prophetic revelation.

What Are We Crossing Over Into?

Back to Jesus' words before the storm: *"Let us cross over to the other side."* This is similar to Israel crossing the Jordan River into their Promised Land. Our generation is crossing over into a place of contending for nations as our, and thus His, inheritance (see Ps. 2:8).

God will fight for us as never before as we finally unpack our prematurely packed rapture bags and set up shop as salt and light in all of the seven cultural mountains.

In Jesus' very first message, the Sermon on the Mount, He gave us our assignment to reform every area of culture by being salt and light. He basically warned us that whatever parts of the world we wouldn't bring the salt of who He is in and through us, or in other words preserve, they would eventually rot and trample us. The King wants to be received, not just as a ticket to heaven, but He wants His better ways of doing things (His Kingdom) to be infused into every area of culture. The King and His Kingdom are a package deal that cannot be separated. When Jesus Himself said, "Repent, the Kingdom is at hand," it was *Him* who was at hand.

Matthew 6:33 tells us to *"seek **first** the kingdom of God,"* not because we are to seek the Kingdom above seeking God, but because seeking the Kingdom *is* seeking God. The King and His Kingdom come together. You can't just have a personal "you and Jesus" relationship and it be enough. He comes with His Kingdom way of doing everything, everywhere and that is what He wants "on earth as it is in heaven."

A Day of Great Deliverance

I prophesied that 2019 and 2020 were hinge years in history when we would experience the greatest rescue operation since the children of Israel's original Passover—when they were then led through the Red Sea and delivered miraculously from generations of oppression. Not coincidentally, we are literally entering into another Passover soon. Perhaps the "Red C" of our generation (as in coronavirus) will also be parted.

We are currently crossing over into a day of great deliverance. Soon enough, life will be known as before and after these present days. You are living in the greatest shift since the Protestant Reformation 500 years ago—and this shift is even bigger. We are shifting from, "How must I be saved?" to, "How then shall we live?" Be aware of the historical moment and respond accordingly. Respond heroically. The present storm is designed to catapult us, not to destroy us. In the storm of our day, it is as if Haman's gallows, originally prepared for the nations' destruction, are being put around Haman's own neck. As in biblical days, you can expect to see a lot of self-destruction from the hidden armies that surround us.

Chapter 3

Roaring Justice and Raging Hope

I released the following prophetic word for the year of 2020 before the coronavirus and other challenges surfaced as a storm:

> *The mirth of the wicked is brief, the joy of the godless lasts but a moment. …***The heavens will expose his guilt;*** *the earth will rise up against him* (Job 20:5, 27 NIV).*

> *May the God of hope fill you with all joy and peace as you trust in him, so that you may overflow with*

hope by the power of the Holy Spirit
(Romans 15:13 NIV).

There is much going on and it's a challenge to only report what God says to report on. It has always been most important to receive reporting directives from the Lord, as His truth often seemingly omits important realities. The ten spies thought it was important to report on the astronomical challenges that they assumed the giants in the land would present to the children of Israel. In contrast, Caleb thought it was best to report only on the "milk and honey" of Canaan, totally minimizing the giants in the land, except to say of them, "They will be bread for us." Forty years later he was proven to be right—the oversized enemies, though theoretically daunting, ended up being just a forgettable "snack." The God-ordained circumcision Israel had to experience after crossing the Jordan River ended up being a much more significant event than the totality of resistance of all the giants.

Today we have a similar scenario. We are close enough to a present Promised Land to see the actual size and layout of the enemy. We comparatively are "as grasshoppers" to what is straight ahead in our paths. If we get into comparing us versus them, then all courage will depart. (Note that I was acknowledging a greater-than-us enemy.)

However, when you (as Caleb did) compare the enemy versus our God, the enemy so pales in comparison, he is dismissible. The swamp, the deep state, Soros' Open Society agenda, the Illuminati, Freemasons, Bilderburgs, CFR, organized sex traffickers, etc. are altogether a laughable resistance when compared to our God. I mean truly laughable! (See Psalm 2:4.) These all presently occupy the Promised Land of the tops of the seven mountains—media, economy, government, education, family, arts and entertainment, and religion. We will not enter Promised Land territory by studying and trying to dismantle the evil that occupies culture. We will enter the Promised Land of the seven mountains of cities and nations by studying and reflecting who God is in each mountain. The difference between the two approaches is enormous and the absolute game-changer.

2020 Corrective Lenses: God in the Equation

Many who follow the prophetic understand that, based on the Hebraic calendar, the last decade has been all about seeing. This prophetic emphasis on *seeing* is because *that* is the entire key to victory. Battles are won and lost at the point of observance—not at the point of engagement. Caleb saw God as supreme and the giants as "bread for us." Once you *see* God in the equation the enemy *always* seems smaller. David's initial observation of Goliath was a belittling, "Who is this uncircumcised Philistine?" Why? Because, as David said, Goliath had defied the armies of the living God. Being able to see the juxtaposition between God and the enemy fueled his easy, anticlimactic beheading of Goliath. David's biggest challenge of the day was not Goliath—that was his piece-of-cake assignment. David's biggest challenge of the day was, in fact, the attempted shutdown by an envious older brother who called for David to go back to watching his "few little sheep" (see 1 Sam. 17:28).

Similarly today, the seven mountains/salt and light/reformation of nations message is under assault by the "older brothers" (old wineskins and denominations) who want to chase us all back to just watching our "few little sheep"—even as they give up more time and more territory to the Goliath criminals on each of the seven mountains. Some have erroneously interpreted that David is Jesus, and that we win when He returns. Jesus has said we are David and we win when we *rise up* in *His* strength.

> *The God of Peace will crush Satan under your feet [our feet!] shortly* (Romans 16:20).

Romans 8:19 tells us that creation itself groans and travails, not for Jesus to return, but for the Davids to arise. Yes, it is God who does it—but it is "Christ *in us*" that is the hope of glory. Yes, God provides all the meaningful power, but He does it when we engage with Him. God did provide the supernatural power for Goliath to be killed—but it was David's ability to see God that activated him. God had the power over the enemy the entire previous 40 days of Goliath's siege but was not going to intervene until someone could first see that and then be moved by what they saw. It is *not*, "God helps those who help themselves," but rather God helps those who properly see Him and thus bring Him into their fight.

See the Two Ditches

There are two ditches to avoid. On one side of the road is the ditch of "in the millennium—one day God—after the rapture" perspective. That is a disempowering ditch that is the old guards' territory-ceding narrative. David's older brother Eliab was never going to be a part of anything other than

fearful survivorship. His kingdom foot-
print was always going to be small. Eliab
was always going to just wait for the "rapture" of his day, and he was always going
to be irritated by the whippersnapper who
thought that the goodness of God could be
seen in the land of the living (see Ps. 27:13).

The ditch on the other side of the road is
self-determinism and self-empowerment. It
says, "God is not going to do anything and
so *we* had better unite and do what needs
to be done because that's how God does
things." This is just as dangerous of a ditch
and it is delusional self-empowerment.
Some proponents of the seven mountains
perspective tend toward this approach as
the cure to the other ditch—but it's just
another ditch. Neither Caleb nor David
was mighty because he believed in himself
or even in Israel's ability to unite and defeat

the enemy. Their gifting was in seeing God and His accompanying narrative—not in their type-A, self-deterministic personality.

When you are *seeing* properly (20/20 vision), everyone is in proper perspective—you, the enemy, and God. *You* have participation. The enemy is the least important detail, but his comparative size *to us* is designed to shock us out of self-help and into a search for co-laboring with God. The God-view is the most important. He is neither absent nor totally accomplishing everything without you. He fights for you, but your battle is responsive obedience that shows you see Him. Without Him you can do nothing. With Him all things are possible.

Roaring Justice and Raging Hope

Justice continues as a major theme, as it has been the last few years—but is now to the next level of progressive intensity. The theme of justice will roar in our nation and then around the world as our God's heart for the used and abused is made evident before all. Justice is not the opposite of mercy, but rather justice is the display of God's mercy on the abused and downtrodden. It is when a line is drawn in the sand against evildoers where there is no more mercy for them apart from wholesale and immediate repentance. The execution of this kind of public justice causes hope to ignite and rage against all doubt, unbelief, and limited thinking. In 2020 and beyond, raging hope will burn up disappointment and delay and it will secure our hearts in a big, good, and present God.

Job 20 is very relevant for 2020. At the beginning of this chapter I already mentioned verses 5 and 27. What I will now say I release as a prophetic word over all those who represent "the swamp" of every nation. This is next in 2020.

Though the pride of the wicked reaches to the heavens and their heads touch the clouds, yet they will vanish forever, thrown away like their own dung. They will fade like a dream and not be found. They will vanish like a vision in the night. His children must make amends to the poor. His own hands must give back his wealth. He will spit out the riches he swallowed; God will make his stomach vomit them up. What he toiled for he must give back uneaten; he will not enjoy the profit from his trading. For he has oppressed the poor and left them destitute; he cannot save himself by his treasure. His prosperity will not endure. In the midst of his plenty, distress will overtake him, the full force of misery will come upon him. God will vent His burning anger against him and rain down His blows upon him. The heavens will expose his guilt and the earth will rise up against him (from Job 20:6-27).

In 2020, another line in the sand will be drawn against organized darkness in the seven mountains of society. When this kind of deep justice takes place, the effect among the people is to release abundant, raging hope. A working definition for real hope is "the expectation of good from God in every area of life." Seeing deep darkness come to justice promotes a growing, hope-filled expectation for life in general. It confirms that there is a right and wrong and it confirms that God looks out for the abused and downtrodden. It confirms specifically that God cares enough, is involved enough, and is big enough to address what is too big for us. Beginning in 2020, let justice roar and let hope rage out of control until His Kingdom comes in its fullness.

Chapter 4

Prophetic Insights from the Chiefs'
Super Bowl Win

I frequently experience God speaking to me through sports events. If God can cause "rocks to cry out" (see Luke 19:40) with His narrative, then He can certainly cause the stats from a nationally viewed game to "cry out" with important navigational understanding for the season we're in. Most of this chapter is taken from a prophetic word I released right after the 2020 Super Bowl (*before* significant attention to the virus), which highlights some key things God is speaking to us.

The Kansas City Chiefs' 31-20 Super Bowl victory over the San Francisco 49ers is full of amazing prophetic messages. Every name, number, date, and time has something to add. I will not go through them all because sometimes more is not better, but can diminish attention on the main things that the Lord would have us focus on. The main message is clear—we have entered into a new day for the Kingdom of God and its advancement on planet earth. The next ones who will be promoted and advanced are those who understand His narrative for the nations.

A Time of Jubilee

It's a good sign that both of these teams were in the Super Bowl. It's a noteworthy accomplishment, even by the losing team. Both speak into a jubilee time of prosperity through debt release. (See Leviticus 25 with a special note on verse 8 regarding "forty-nine years" and verse 11 "the fiftieth year.")

There was also a similar prophetic message from Baton Rouge (meaning Red Pole) based LSU Tigers winning the College Football National Championship, led by record-breaking player of the year Joseph Burrow. As we remember Joseph in the Old Testament, he was responsible for turning a forecast of a dire famine into unprecedented prosperity that blessed all nations. Genesis 41:57 tells us that *"all countries came to Joseph."* This is something only God could orchestrate.

The 49ers refer to the gold rush in California. The biblical time of jubilee had a focus on the 49th and 50th year—as I pointed out from Leviticus 25. It was repeatedly noted that Kansas City's last Super Bowl win was 50 years ago. Also, their star quarterback, Pat Mahomes, is noted as the only player to ever throw for 50 touchdowns in both the pros and in college. So 49 and 50 were both highlighted—although that the "50" team won is an even better message. This confirms that we are not about to have a jubilee, but we are presently in a time of jubilee.

At the time of the Super Bowl, a jubilee/Joseph reality seemed quite evident in how our nation's economy was doing. Although it is currently very challenged in the midst of this storm, I believe I have seen an upcoming 35,000 on the stock market, and long term, the worldwide economic upgrade will be most significant. The coming economic shifts will be staggering and unprecedented (this last sentence I released while the DOW Jones was at 29,000). The world has lived essentially under lack and in survival mode, but will begin to learn to live in overall prosperity.

The Test of Abundance

Many have experienced the test of lack, but it's an entirely new thing to experience the test of abundance. Lucifer failed the test of abundance. This may come as a surprise, but God doesn't really have a person or a people He can trust until they've passed the test of abundance. Abundance tests a spirit in an entirely different way and is more revealing of who a person is. The world's wealthy, under some definitions, make up essentially 5% of the population. As this extended time of jubilee grows into a Jubilee Age, we'll see the wealthy suddenly become

15% and then 25% and then 50% and then 70% of the population.

This is the coming reality for all sheep nations (see Matt. 25:32-33). I and two other prophets were shown in the same week, independently of each other, that there will be 153 sheep nations. Chuck Pierce was taken in the spirit and shown the 153 nations. I was given revelation that same week out of John 21 where, in verse 11, Peter caught 153 large fish after tossing his net "on the right side of the boat." Jesus then told him in verse 17, *"Feed My sheep."* There will be 153 sheep nations—but all are invited to be so. Perhaps this seems impossible, but once you get a first one it moves quicker than you think. The impossible becomes probable and then certain.

The percentage of the wealthy not surpassing 70% is indicative of the fact that

Jesus said, "the poor you always have with you." We can always choose less than He offers. We can be so broken or deceived that we're not able to receive what He has for us. He has never revealed Himself as the God of "just enough." From His best Old Testament friends being very wealthy (Abraham, Joseph, David, etc.) to how He enticed Israel into their Promised Land *("a land which flows with milk and honey,"* you shall be *"the head and not the tail," "you shall lend to many nations, but you shall not borrow,"* I will give you "cities which you did not build")—we see His heart to trust us with abundance (Num. 14:8; Deut. 28:12-13; 6:10). Then, in the person of Jesus, all of His provision miracles were above and beyond. His first miracle at Cana was 150–180 gallons of the best wine, just to help finish celebrating a wedding. Peter, upon obeying Jesus' instruction to cast on the right side, almost had his nets destroyed and greatly challenged his boat's capacity to contain it all. Jesus fed 5,000 with 12 baskets left over. We see these kinds of miracles again and again through Jesus. Abundance is His trademark. His provision was always pressed down, shaken together, and running over. Remember, if poverty were a virtue, it would exist in heaven. It doesn't.

Don't forget the truth of 2 Chronicles 20:20, which speaks of hearkening to His prophets so that you will prosper. I am giving you a prophetic decree—the test of prosperity is next. It will be many decades before it finishes maturing. Any lead-up economic shaking or contradiction is only designed to facilitate that reality. For those wanting things to fall apart so Jesus can come—deal with it, this is next. He comes *to* us and *through* us before He comes *for* us.

We are not "caught up" with Him in the sky as a rescue operation for a beleaguered Bride of Christ—but only as a fulfillment and celebration of something accomplished. The present rescue operation is so we can advance with our earthly assignment of receiving His Kingdom on the earth and filling the whole earth with the knowledge of the glory of the Lord. That is how His Bride (the church) makes herself ready for her Bridegroom.

Chief of the Mountains

The Chiefs won on 2/2 of 2020. It was coach Andy Reid's 222nd victory. That week 22, 222, and 2222s were highlighted to me everywhere. Remember, if "rocks will cry out" if truth/praise is suppressed, so can numbers (see Luke 19:40). The invisible things of Him get revealed through His creation (see Rom. 1:20). He makes earth's newsworthy matters a "Bible" of truth that supports the written Bible. This is why He can say, "so that they are without excuse."

> *Now it will come about that in the last days the mountain of the house of the Lord will be established as **chief** of the mountains...and all the nations will stream to it* (Isaiah 2:2 NASB).

This verse is the original foundational scripture for the seven mountain message as well as my first book, *The Seven Mountain Prophecy*. It speaks of a time when not only individuals are saved but entire nations seek solutions from activated reformers from the house of the Lord. This can be called revival, but it's much greater than that. We've never seen reformation and transformation like what's coming. So, for lack of an example, we tend to call everything we are waiting for *revival*. The upgrade in vocabulary and in understanding is mainly important so that we don't settle for less than what He's doing. In order for the house of the Lord to be established as *chief* of all mountains we have to finally value our mission to be salt and light on the seven mountains—that is a reformation assignment. As Jesus said in Matthew 5:16, *"Let your light so **shine** before men, that they **may see**...."* This is God at work in the public places of society. That, in essence, is the seven-mountain mandate—revival *and* reformation. The full process is a renaissance.

> *Suddenly, there was a sound from heaven like the **roaring** of a mighty windstorm, and it filled the house where they were sitting* (Acts 2:2 NLT).

This verse will have many manifestations. This is what birthed the New Testament church and what is now birthing us into the Kingdom Age of our day. The mighty rushing wind that's roaring in at this time isn't just for the purpose of having good church meetings, but also to address the justice matters that revived reformers know must be addressed. Great hope (the expectation of good from God) will be its result.

Keys to the Highest Positions

> *I will give him the key to the house of David—the **highest position** in the royal court. When he opens doors, no one will be able to close them, when he closes doors, no one will be able to open them* (Isaiah 22:22 NLT).

This verse speaks of a key that opens and closes and is connected to the highest position. This connects to how God is using President Donald Trump. It's no coincidence that he is Commander-in-Chief. His name *Donald* essentially means "chief ruler." I'm still shocked by the believers who can't discern that Trump is God-sent. It was understandable at first as he came in somewhat disguised, but now that his stands and legislation have proven his motivations over and over, it is indisputably obvious that Trump is advancing a Kingdom agenda.

If you've been tempted to judge President Trump for things prior to his presidency and ignore that he is the most pro-life, pro-Israel, pro-religious freedom, pro-poor, pro-enslaved by human trafficking president in history—then I'm concerned that perhaps you've been affected by the deep state's agenda and the false media's narrative. It's not too late to wake up and see what God is doing.

The Chiefs' Super Bowl win is yet another way God is letting us know that the Commander-in-Chief is going to continue winning. Of course, God is our ultimate Commander-in-Chief, but to not recognize when He sends and activates a key Kingdom asset is offensive to Him—though He is used to that. He verbally chastised Israel for not recognizing when He sent (imperfect) prophets, and it has never been a small deal to Him when we refuse His messengers, prophets, and kings. Trump is as divinely orchestrated of a messenger as any biblical messenger was.

God loves us unconditionally, but we displease Him if we haven't recognized His intentionality in establishing Donald J. Trump as president. God has been displeased with both Republicans and Democrats, so don't think this is political at all. In fact, I think President Trump might one day tell us he strongly considered running as a Democrat. If the Democrats hadn't veered so radically to the left, he really might have. Now get ready though—Trump is going to get his Acts 2:2 visitation, and he's going to get louder. The Holy Spirit has a roar too— especially when defending the defenseless.

Kansas City 31 and Proverbs 31

Kansas City winning the Super Bowl with a score of 31 is no coincidence. Proverbs 31 is the well-known biblical reference to the virtuous woman. The whole chapter is worth going over in detail when we consider the virtuous woman as a representation of Christ's Bride (His church) here on earth.

The word for "virtuous" in verse 10 is the Hebrew word *chayill*, which means "strength, might, efficiency, wealth, army, force, power, riches, substance." Put all those words together and it gives us an understanding of what's required to defeat the enemy. We must arise and shine into those virtues to overcome victoriously.

> *The thief does not come except to steal, and to kill, and to destroy. I have come that they may have life, and that they may have it more abundantly* (John 10:10).

Remember the halftime 10-10 stalemate? That's where many of us have been and where part of 2020 seems to be taking us. The Chiefs couldn't get past 10 until the last half of the last quarter. This year may have its challenges, but we're destined for a big win. The new 31 score is now declared over your life, and with it, take on the new responsibilities related to issues of justice.

> *Speak up for those who cannot speak for themselves;* ***ensure justice f****or those being crushed. Yes, speak up for the poor and helpless, and see that they get* ***justice*** (Proverbs 31:8-9 NLT).

A justice focus always goes beyond what we think of as traditional revival. If we want to score enough to be on the winning side, then we must embrace reformation and our seven-mountain assignments.

The 2020 Election: Vote, Pray, Love

> *She extends a helping hand to the poor and opens her arms to the needy* (Proverbs 31:20 NLT).

The Super Bowl final score was 31-20, which connects us to our reformation assignment of love in action on the seven mountains of culture. Love that is expressed as practical solutions to real problems in society is what is required to post a winning score—personally and as a nation.

I was given a shocking set of numbers from the Lord as it relates to the coming 2020 presidential election. Consider this—I heard that President Trump could win with either 51%, 57%, or 71% of the vote. If God's people prioritized *voting*, then he could win with 51%; if we added the priority of *praying*, then he could win with 57%; if we would truly *be love in action*, then we could see a 71% win. This last one is the one we are often least committed to, but could do the most.

It's specifically important to love across racial lines and not only love those like yourself. I believe part of the reason much of the black community and the Latino community have traditionally rejected the Republican Party is that they have never felt the love. Many white Republicans have typically tended to think it's enough to be pro-life and that it's the highest, all-encompassing moral ground possible. It's not good enough. If we don't reach across racial lines, seeking to hear first before speaking, we'll have another squeaker election. It wouldn't hurt us to be at the forefront of championing many other important justice issues that those unlike us face. A Proverbs 31 virtuous church will do that.

All Her Household Are Clothed in Red

Proverbs 31:21 says of the virtuous woman, *"all her household is clothed with scarlet* (red)."

Red has been the key color I have spoken of for some time. It was obviously the Chiefs' color. LSU was from Baton Rouge, meaning "Red Pole." Justify, the horse that won the Triple Crown, wore red as its dominant color. The Alabama Crimson Tide has been highlighted many times in the last few years. We are seeing red highlighted over and over. Yes, the Republican color is red, but all the red isn't really about the Republican Party. It's about the redeeming blood of Jesus setting the agenda for everything presently transpiring on planet earth. He paid for us with His blood and we are His. Now He is coming to us—not to whisk us to heaven, but to create a place of habitation on earth.

Her husband is well known at the city gates, where he sits with the other civic leaders (Proverbs 31:23 NLT).

If we understand that our husband is Jesus, it yet again confirms our reformation call. The New Testament word for church, *ekklesia*, was not a religious word. It was essentially civic leaders serving on the seven mountains, or at their city gates. This is where He builds His church and the gates of hell will not prevail against it (see Matt. 16:18).

> *Reward her for all she has done. Let her deeds publicly declare her praise* (Proverbs 31:31 NLT).

> *Let your light so shine before men, that they may see your good works and glorify your Father in heaven* (Matthew 5:16).

The mountain of the house of the Lord is established as *chief* of the mountains when we "score the winning 31 points" from

Proverbs 31. Prosperity and rewards are prepared for us, but He wants our activity to stretch beyond private or church life. Reformation is about the Kingdom going *public*.

Final Words on Super Bowl

The Chiefs won on the 33rd day of the year with 333 days remaining because it's leap year. The storm is not designed to take us out but to catapult us forward. When Jesus was 33, the events in Acts 2 took place and the Holy Spirit invaded the earth as never before. Jeremiah 33:3 says, *"Call to Me, and I will answer you, and show you great and mighty things, which you do not know."*

LIV was the logo for Super Bowl 54 in Roman numerals. Isaiah 54 begins with, *"Sing, O barren,"* because fruitfulness is coming. The LIV also communicates *live*—this is a time to contend for *life* everywhere. Agendas of death are being identified and routed.

Star quarterback/MVP Pat Mahomes was 24 years old, a highlighted number this year. This connects to Psalm 24, which speaks of ancient doors opening so that the King of Glory may come in.

I haven't covered the Hunt family who own the Chiefs, but I'd at least like to point out the fact that they honor Jesus above everything. I believe the troubling halftime show was to remind us of the work ahead and why we can't just keep our light in the four walls of the church. Obviously, money drives things; therefore, we can become the sponsors that provide better options, or we can constantly complain about what is shown. When God said we would be the head and not the tail, we must remember that "tails" always powerlessly lament; "heads" always dictate. Darkness will always prevail where light refuses to shine. Now is the time for Isaiah 2:2—let's arise with the love and light of who God is and His better ways in every area of society.

Chapter 5

Better Than We Can Imagine

This year the way becomes more and more clear moving forward. The story of Israel's departure from Egypt through the Red Sea in Exodus 14 is particularly relevant. This is a time that's as historical and significant for the United States and the nations as the biblical Exodus was for Israel.

I began speaking this word in 2018, but as is often the case, there's a time when you experience a very specific moment when what the Lord is saying manifests. I believe we'll look back and see that the literal Passover of 2020 was our Exodus 14 reality. We're in the midst of applying the blood of Jesus to our households as a killer virus rages. Next, we'll march out of a long, multi-generational bondage to a sick, ruling elite, and the Red Sea that we thought might take us out will instead have propelled us forward.

The scope and scale of shift and change cannot be overstated. We are at the threshold of the greatest breakthrough ever as a nation, and it may feel precarious at times. This is a rescue operation and a deliverance of the highest magnitude. A hundred (or more) years of murky and distorted history will be clarified. Many news-making stories of the past century were not as reported and much of that will be progressively made clear. This is a process that will take a few years, but there's no mistaking the central role that 2020 will have carried in it all.

A Great Day of Deliverance

In the original story described in Exodus 14, the children of Israel left Egypt only to find themselves with the impossible predicament of the Red Sea before them and Pharaoh's army chasing them from behind. This day didn't seem at all like a day they would fondly remember and sing of forever—though that's exactly what happened. It seemed more like a day that would live in infamy with certain destruction either from the Egyptian oppressors or the waves of the Red Sea.

Similarly, today the enemies seem daunting—once you actually know about them. Today our Red Sea is the swamp of entrenched corruption that we find ourselves facing in the world. (Interestingly, some scholars believe the Red Sea was actually more of a reedy swamp.) Pharaoh and his forces similarly represent the church's history of being the tail rather than the head, continually being chased rather than leading the way. We've been conditioned to expect any potentially good outcome to be sabotaged—and "breakthrough" always seems quite elusive. We're in another day now that won't necessarily be easy to go through, but it will be a great day of deliverance.

The children of Israel were being pursued by Pharaoh and 600 chariots. The 600 represents man's best showing of organized power, as 6 is the number of man. The children of Israel had hundreds of years of some level of bondage to Egypt. The Red Sea was in between them and the open path to freedom to worship and to their Promised Land. Something had to give.

Moses was instructed to raise his rod and with *that* the Red Sea would part and allow them to cross over. He did this, and as Israel crossed on dry land the pursuing Egyptians could be seen bearing down. As soon as Israel was through, Moses raised his rod and the Red Sea waters that formerly served the Egyptians' purposes of control now turned on them and drowned them all (see Exod. 14:28).

This dynamic is something we're walking through now. There are power brokers of society who have thought the future was theirs to script according to their controlling interests. The great surprise at who actually rules has only just begun to slap them in the face as our God, for His own name's sake, interjects His plans and purposes into history. The church has been in arrested development through its premature focus on exiting the planet. This has caused an abandonment of the seven mountains of society. We relinquished our mandate to be salt and light in all areas of culture, which gave the enemy an extended period of time to become deeply embedded in positions of power and influence. God is now moving with those who are awake, positioning us for the greater awakening that's ensuing.

Exodus 14:25 says the Lord *"took off their chariot wheels,"* leaving the Egyptians to conclude that God was fighting against them. Verse 30 is particularly poignant and says, *"The Lord saved Israel that day out of the hand of the Egyptians."* These words speak prophetically to us even today.

God Will Remove the Wheels of the Deep State

Just because many conspiracy theorists believe in the deep state doesn't mean it doesn't exist. It does exist. In fact, the term "conspiracy theory" was invented by the conspirers to stop further inquiry. However, the deep state is much like the chariot wheels of the Egyptian army. They are wheels or circles of syndicated power that run over the common people with the goals and plots of the oppressors. God is going to make them as irrelevant today as they were in the Red Sea crossing. Their own wheels got them stuck in the mud of their own Red Sea and ultimately led to their demise. What they thought would hem in the children of Israel actually propelled them and instead caused their own destruction. Truly another case of Haman's own gallows being used against him.

And the Lord Saved the United States

Even as it was said in verse 30, *"The Lord saved Israel,"* so it will be realized that we too have been similarly saved and are the recipients of a great work of *divine deliverance*. This will be something important as we move forward—as we sometimes confuse the fact that we do have a responsibility from our end to do *something*—as the proof that it's all up to us. We do need to, by faith, apply the blood to our homes. We do need to commit to leaving behind all that is the bondage of Egypt. But once again, the battle is the Lord's. Only He can part the Red Sea and leave it dry for us while drowning our enemy in it. What a mighty God we serve!

Israel Will Remain Central

It should only seem logical, if we're valuing this intervention from God based on the Jewish calendar for Passover (April 2020), that Israel is established as a preeminent point of reference in the world and in Kingdom affairs. There are so many things regarding Israel that God will be working on in 2020 and beyond. There are surreptitious elements within Israel's intelligence community that are going to be exposed, which will become an important national and even international matter. Exposure of corruption, especially sexual, is going to be something God is going after, while simultaneously judging the outside nations that attempt to do Israel harm. He will be the perfect parent to Israel during these days, both correcting and protecting—and we are to understand and cooperate with His heart toward His initial covenant people. Israel is central to God's master storytelling of the ages, and that's worth never losing sight of. He'll be ever-rescuing and delivering Israel because He who began a good work will complete it perfectly.

God Hears the Cry of China

The coronavirus pandemic birthed out of Wuhan, China has spotlighted the nation before the world in perhaps a negative light (depending on how deceitful the media you listen to has been). Some have appropriately called it the CCP virus, as in the China Communist Party virus. We've also become aware of how that ruling party has managed to infiltrate the tops of the seven mountains of China's culture and has partnered with darkness. Present information seems to signal that they've targeted President Trump and the United States. There will be consequences. Truly it could be easy to view the Red Sea of our day being a Red C, as in the Communist Party of China. This Red C will also be parted.

Though China officially reports their Christian population as being under 100 million, that's clearly a fake number. They don't count those under age 18, as they presently aren't legally allowed to be Christians according to their new law, nor do they count the underground church. In 2006, their own head of the Religious Affairs Bureau reported in a closed-door meeting in Peking University that there were 110 million Protestants. I won't state his name in case it would endanger him. With the annual growth he reported at the time, that would make Protestants number 234 million in 2020—essentially by their own admission. You can add millions of Catholics to that number, making 250 million very reasonable. Mainly, I know the Lord spoke to me that there were well over 200 million followers of Jesus in China and my own research has confirmed that.

Even today the Lord allowed me to hear in my spirit the cry of China from those who follow Jesus there. The cry of China before the Lord is loud and "un-ignorable." If there are 250 million believers in China then it's the nation with the most believers on the planet. This great day of deliverance is for China as well. God has heard their cry.

Over the last few months, President Xi (perhaps a puppet?) has recognized the threat of this exploding Christian presence and has brought draconian restrictions on all religious activity. This has greatly increased the persecution in China as many churches have been shut down and even destroyed, pastors jailed, and over 7,000 crosses knocked off of church buildings.

A *New York Post* headline recently said, "How China's Xi Jinping Destroyed

Religion and Made Himself God." February 1, 2020 another 41 restrictions were added to religious practices. God has heard the cry of His oppressed in China and is going to create a Passover reality for them as well. Whether China's day of deliverance coincides perfectly with our timetable in the United States, there is no doubt that what happens here and now is shortly going to positively reverberate there.

I was shown a picture of President Xi poking God in the eye through his recent measures. If there was ever a time not to do that, it's now. God has come to set His people free and especially free to worship. God is right now saying to President Xi, "Let My people go." There are always consequences to ignoring that command. The CCP is celebrating 70 years of ruling China. I don't believe they'll make it to a 75th anniversary.

Though this can be shocking to process, I believe there are 30 million Christians within the Chinese Communist Party. When I was in China a few years ago, I heard this saying several times, "If all the Christians in the CCP left the CCP, there would be no more CCP." While this may have been an exaggeration, I believe that 30 million is a realistic number. The Lord showed me He had millions near the head of the CCP and mostly as His "sleeper cells." Many have been promoted because they carry the light and favor of Jesus. They will soon be activated by God. I see a future where America and China partner to be a blessing to the world. I see a picture of the Golden Gate Bridge and America as the support structure on one end and China on the other end. This will be a Golden Gate of provision for the nations as these two superpowers together create and release world opportunities to prosper.

Navigating the New Era

As we move forward in the midst of the current storm, I'd like to encourage you to remember these five important truths:

1. The good things God spoke to us about 2020 and beyond, He is still saying.

2. This is not the end of the world, only an end that allows for the beginning of a new era of promise.

3. It's truly the end for multiple generations of evil in high places as they collide with unprecedented justice.

4. Final end-time scenarios are not for our lifetime—so hope, dream, plan, and act accordingly. Think 100 years.

5. Stop listening to any voice that instills fear or removes hope. Endless possibilities is our new mantra.

Rescued and Propelled

New technologies are about to abound. New energy forms that eventually, and maybe sooner than later, give us all free energy are about to be seen. Many cures for diseases have been suppressed and will soon be released into society. I believe both cancer and AIDS already have cures presently on earth and will finally be brought to the light of day. True Kingdom projects that have been sabotaged for years are about to be fully funded. Abundance for reformation of society is next. This year, 2020, will be the great hinge year for us, ushering us into a new era. Children born in 2020 are going to be wired for the tops of the mountains. They'll be part of a Justice League generation that will occupy the places of influence, bringing the light of Jesus and the empowerment of the Holy Spirit to everything. We are first being rescued. Then we will be propelled. The future is not only better than you think—it's better than you can imagine.

Post Word

What Does This Mean for Each of Us?

Elizabeth Enlow

In this book Johnny referred to Mark 4 and the story of Jesus and His disciples in the boat during a storm. It's relevant to note that, right before they got in the boat, Jesus was teaching them and others a lesson about the Kingdom of God. That same day, at the direction of their Teacher, they got in a boat to cross to the other side of the Sea of Galilee. It seems to me that the lesson from earlier in the day actually wasn't over and what they would encounter along the way and once they arrived was a continuation of His very intentional training. I believe this is relevant to us today because we are also in the midst of our own Kingdom training, individually and as potential sheep nations. What felt like an interruption, a crisis, and something that was a distraction from an overall direction and plan was, in fact, a critical part of the bigger picture goal—their discipleship process that would prepare them to be commissioned to demonstrate the very Kingdom He taught and modeled for them.

The disciples' cry is the part of the story that captures my attention, especially in the current storm our generation is weathering. The disciples' question to Jesus was, in essence, "Don't You care?" Like all of us, they attributed their perspective of the nature and character of God to their current circumstance—they were scared and fighting for their lives while Jesus was asleep and unmoved. We can all relate to the idea of being in a storm and wondering, as the disciples did, does God care? Perhaps that's the most common cry of every heart that has ever lived. In contrast, what's quite rare is the reality we are collectively in, in this time in history. Seemingly everyone is in the same storm, and whether we all realize it consciously or not, our Teacher is teaching us. We are headed somewhere on purpose, quite intentional, for a specific reason that we will all be invited into. He has a captive audience.

So what were the disciples crossing over to? As the story unfolds in Mark 5, we're told that they went to the country of the Gadarenes (which means "reward at the end") where they encountered a man with an unclean spirit. Jesus delivered him from a legion of demons, then promptly got back in the boat and returned to the other side in order for their lessons to continue. In the same way, we are being escorted by our Teacher through a storm for the purpose of a much bigger lesson and reward than merely the survival of something horrible.

In order to understand the process we are each individually in with God, it's helpful to understand the way Jesus taught. He would teach with stories that were real-life scenarios, using images that meant something personal to them in the context of their culture. He would hide truth that demanded interaction with Him and would necessitate questions, explanations, and conversation with Him and with each other. Not only did He teach them about the Kingdom, but He went out of His way to take them on a high-stakes adventure, gave them an up-close live demonstration of what He had verbally taught them, and eventually commissioned and activated them into His Kingdom.

What was Jesus modeling for them and what was it that allowed Jesus to rest in the storm, even to the point of sleep? Obviously He did care, because once He was awakened He quickly stopped the storm. I believe Jesus was the best kind of Teacher of all—one who never misses a moment to demonstrate the lesson in the most unforgettable way. He was aware that He was in the middle of training them for something super important that required their faith to be stretched. I think it's fair to say that none of us will ever forget the things we're currently experiencing, and God will not only navigate us through this storm, but we'll learn and grow in incredible ways that will redeem all that seems lost and allow us to respond with greater faith in the next storm.

As Johnny and I have spent the last decade traveling and interacting with the global church, we've given our lives to awakening, equipping, and connecting reformers—followers of Jesus who know they were created to change the world by bringing the Kingdom of heaven to earth through practical solutions and real expressions of the love of God in all seven mountains of culture in every nation. Our ministry, Restore7, has embraced the mission of expanding your impact on the world by expanding your perspective of God. It's our hope that, as you read prophetic insights like this one and interact with our other resources, you find greater understanding of not only the bigger picture of what God is doing, but also your unique place within it.

If this hopeful perspective resonates with you, then we'd especially like to invite you to join a global community of reformers called RISE. RISE stands for Reformers Influencing Society Every day. This is a community of disciples-in-training, like you, who are about to graduate into all the things God's sons and daughters are being specifically trained for throughout the challenges of life at this time in history.

Jesus is a Teacher who's all about relationships—our relationship with Him and with each other. Everything He did was in the context of relationship. He's doing no less with each of us, collectively and individually, today. The RISE community meets in small groups in public places and online for the purpose of Kingdom impact in the context of relationships with God and with one another. Our focus is to be the church outside of the four walls of the church.

If you're interested, it's easy to join simply by completing the RISE Online Video Course or by reading *RISE: A Handbook for Reformers on the Seven Mountains*, which was intentionally designed to get everyone within the community on the same page, contending for the same things. The RISE Global Community is accessed through an app that will be available in 2020. You can find out all the details at www.RISE7.org. To learn more about our ministry go to www.Restore7.org.

About the Authors

Johnny and Elizabeth Enlow are social reformers at heart, as well as international speakers and authors of *The Seven Mountain Prophecy, The Seven Mountain Mantle, Rainbow God, The Seven Mountain Renaissance, Becoming A Superhero, God in Every Season,* and *RISE: A Handbook for Reformers on the Seven Mountains.* As ones focused on the reformation of the seven primary areas of culture, they are spiritual mentors to many in Media, Arts and Entertainment, Government, Family, Religion, Economy, and Education.

Johnny and Elizabeth are spiritual parents to many throughout the nations, as well as their son, Eric and 4 daughters—Promise, Justice, Grace, and Glory—and grandparents to one grandson, so far. Together they are co-founders of Restore7 ministry, which globally serves influencers in every area of society. Their current focus is on projects including an app called RISE which serves as a connecting point for a global community of reformers, producing a documentary about the Peruvian economic miracle, and launching several new nonprofits including a Christian government training center in Washington, DC. Their passion is to awaken our generation to the reality of the God of all of life, who not only cares for our souls, but also has practical solutions to offer through His sons and daughters for every problem that exists in society.

Made in the USA
Middletown, DE
20 August 2020